TOW TRUCKS

JEN BESEL

BLACK RABBIT BOOKS

Bolt Jr. is published by Black Rabbit Books
P.O. Box 227, Mankato, Minnesota, 56002.
www.blackrabbitbooks.com
Copyright © 2023 Black Rabbit Books

Michael Sellner, interior designer; Grant Gould, cover designer;
Omay Ayres, photo researcher

All rights reserved. No part of this book may be
reproduced in any form without written permission
from the publisher.

Names: Besel, Jennifer M., author.
Title: Tow trucks / Jen Besel.
Description: Mankato, Minnesota : Black Rabbit Books, [2023] | Series: Bolt jr. Emergency vehicles | Includes bibliographical references and index. | Audience: Ages 6-8. Audience: Grades K-1. | Summary: "Hop in and see how tow trucks jump into action and bring help fast"— Provided by publisher.
Identifiers: LCCN 2019053240 (print) | LCCN 2019053241 (ebook) | ISBN 9781623104658 (library binding) | ISBN 9781644664513 (paperback) | ISBN 9781623104955 (ebook)
Subjects: LCSH: Wreckers (Vehicles)—Juvenile literature.
Classification: LCC TL230.15 .B473 2023 (print) | LCC TL230.15 (ebook) | DDC 629.225—dc23
LC record available at https://lccn.loc.gov/2019053240
LC ebook record available at https://lccn.loc.gov/2019053241

Image Credits
123RF: Danylo Samiylenko, 7; NejroN, 15; Dreamstime: David Touchtone, 8–9; Miwi97, 13; Eastern Suburbs Towing Sydney: ESTS, 15; iStock: Andyqwe, 10–11; bluegame, 15; DNY59, 21; kozmoat98, 14; MarekPiotrowski, Cover; Terryfic3D, 5; millerind.com: Miller Industries, 16–17, 22–23; pro-tow.com: Pro-Tow, 4; Shutterstock: aapsky, 6–7; Aleksandar Malivuk, 14; Bro Studio, 3, 24; David Touchtone, Cover; Jevanto Productions, 12–13; Le Do, 19; LeeAnn White, 19; Macrovector, 1; Mechanik, 10–11; TFoxFoto, 20–21; Thanaporn Pinpart, 19; VOLYK IEVGENII, 14–15; TowForce: Randall C. Resch, 18–19

Contents

Chapter 1
In Action 4

Chapter 2
On the Job 10

Chapter 3
A Look Inside 16

More Information 22

CHAPTER 1

In Action

A **wrecked** car sits on the road. It can't drive. Soon, a tow truck arrives. It lifts the car up. Then the tow truck pulls it away.

wrecked: damaged or destroyed

5

flatbed
about 8 feet
(2 meters)

COMPARING
WIDTHS

There to Help

Tow trucks are helpful vehicles. Cars break down. They get into accidents. When vehicles can't be driven, tow trucks move them.

▶ **full-size pickup truck bed**
about 4 feet (1 m)

PARTS OF A
Tow Truck

wheels

emergency lights

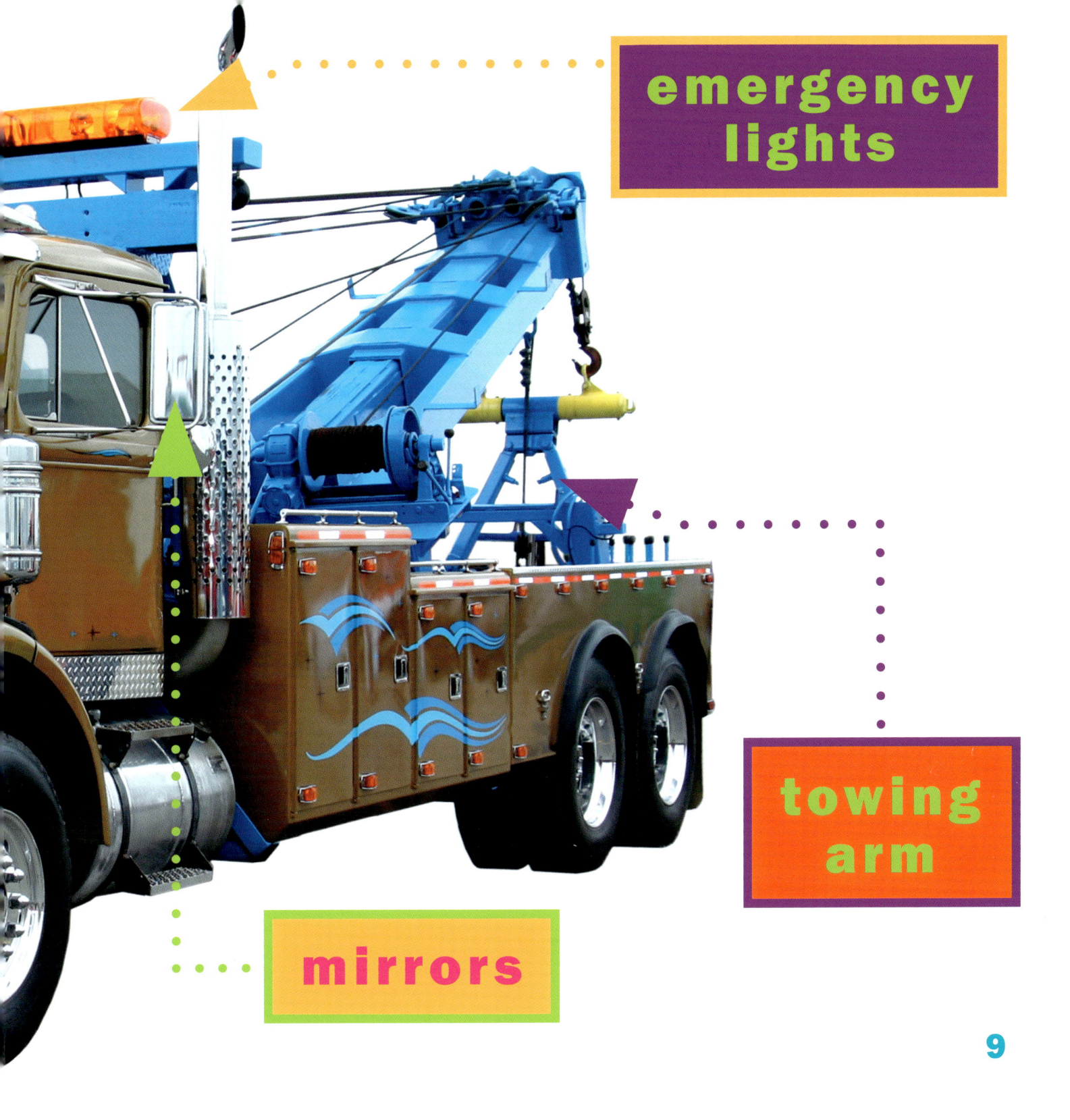

towing arm

mirrors

9

CHAPTER 2

On the Job

There are tow trucks for every job. Flatbed trucks carry cars on them. Wheel-lift trucks pick up one end of a car. Other trucks **haul** big vehicles like buses.

haul: to move something by pulling

FACT
Police call tow trucks to move cars parked where they shouldn't.

12

Not Too Fast!

The fastest tow truck went 109 miles (175 kilometers) per hour. But these trucks don't usually go that fast. They have to follow the **speed limit**. Laws say they can't race through traffic.

speed limit: the fastest speed allowed by law

When Someone Needs a Tow Truck

Step 1
A driver calls a tow truck company for help.

Step 2
The company sends a truck to the location.

Step 3

The truck driver makes sure the area is safe.

Step 4

Then the truck driver loads the car on the truck.

Step 5

The truck pulls the car to a repair shop.

CHAPTER 3

A Look Inside

Inside the cab, drivers have levers and buttons. They connect to the truck's bed or towing arm. The driver uses them to raise or lower equipment.

FACT

Trucks carry fire extinguishers.

| UP
HITCH-
WHEELIFT
DOWN | OUT
HITCH-
WHEELIFT
IN | OUT
WINCH
IN | UP
BODY
TILT
DOWN | BACK
BODY
FORWARD |

BODY BACK FIRST TO CLEAR LOCKS.

212L   DO NOT SLIDE BODY BACK MORE THAN 4 FEET WITH HITCH EXTENDED. SET ENGINE R.P.M. FROM 700-1200 TO OPERATE UNIT.

NOT OPERATE IF ANYONE IS BEHIND THE CARRIER. DO NOT WALK OR STAND BEHIND CARRIER
HILE IN OPERATION. INSPECT VEHICLE, CARRIER, AND WINCH CABLE PRIOR TO DAILY USE. HAVE
PAIRS MADE BEFORE OPERATING CARRIER.

WARNING
DO **NOT** OPERATE UNIT UNLE
THE OWNER'S MANUAL HAS B
READ. USE OF THIS UNIT M
RESULT IN INJURY OR DEATH
VEHICLE OR ITS EQUIPMENT
OPERATED IN AN UNSAFE MAN
OR AN UNPROTECTED AREA.

17

18

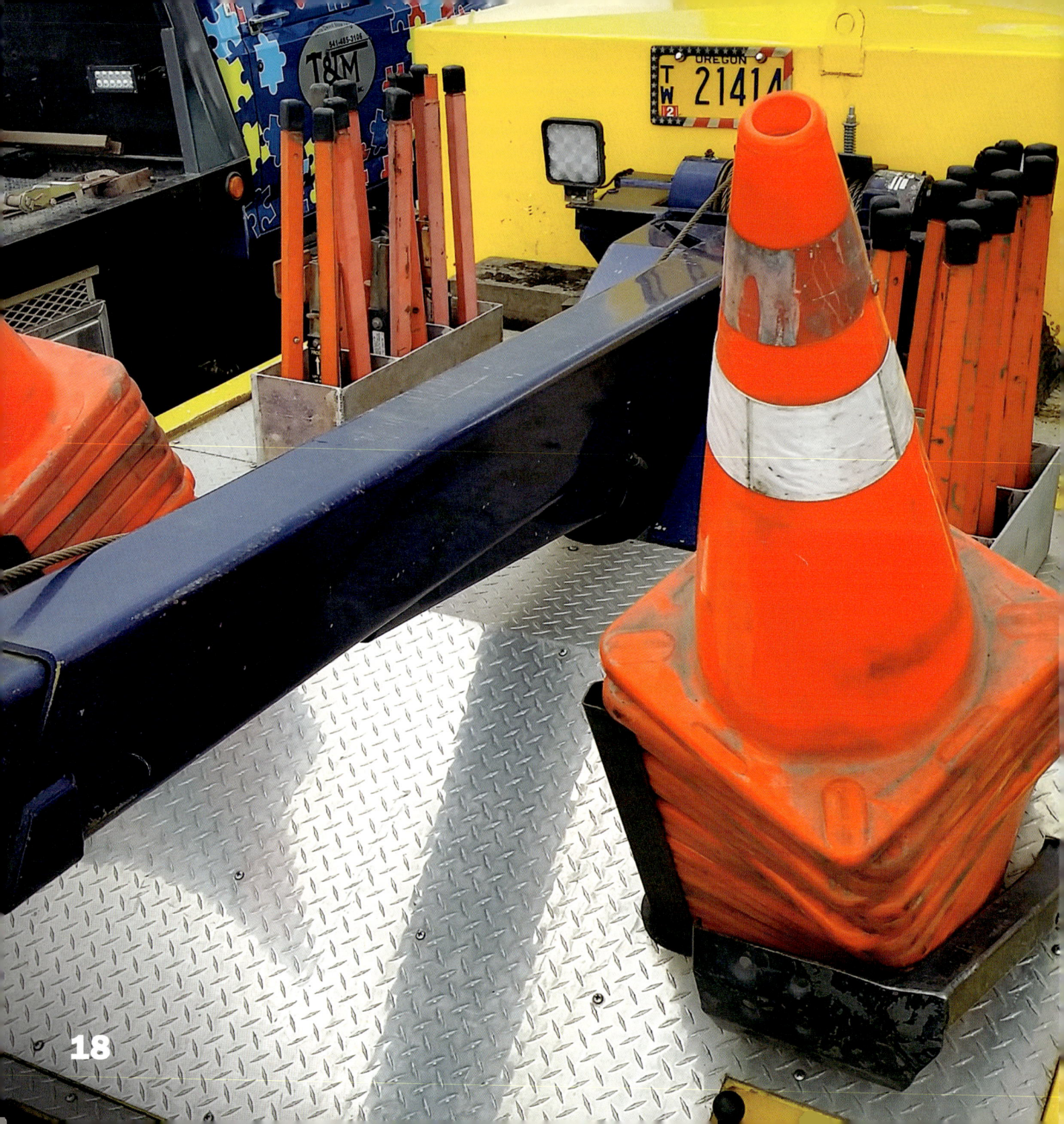

Tools

Drivers bring tools in their trucks too. They bring flashlights. They also bring safety cones. They put those out when they're loading the tow truck.

Other Tow Truck Tools

pry bar   straps    wheel chocks

19

Bonus Facts

The biggest tow trucks cost $1 million.

They were invented in 1916.

There's a tow truck museum in Tennessee.

Tow truck drivers need a special **license**.

license: official permission to do or use something

21

READ MORE/WEBSITES

Pace, Anne Marie. *Sunny's Tow Truck Saves the Day!* New York: Abrams Appleseed, 2019.

Riggs, Kate. *Tow Trucks.* Seedlings. Mankato, MN: Creative Education, 2017.

Zachary, Paul. *Tow Trucks.* Working Trucks. Hallandale, FL: Mitchell Lane Publishers, 2019.

Large Tow Trucks | How It's Made
www.youtube.com/watch?v=FqOUejbG4jg

Tow Truck for Children
www.youtube.com/watch?v=9uc-zUHsz_w

GLOSSARY

haul (HAWL)—to move something by pulling

license (LY-sens)—official permission to do or use something

speed limit (SPEED LIH-mit)—the fastest speed allowed by law

wrecked (REKT)—damaged or destroyed

INDEX

C
costs, 20

F
features, 8–9, 16

S
sizes, 6
speeds, 13

T
tools, 16, 19
types, 10